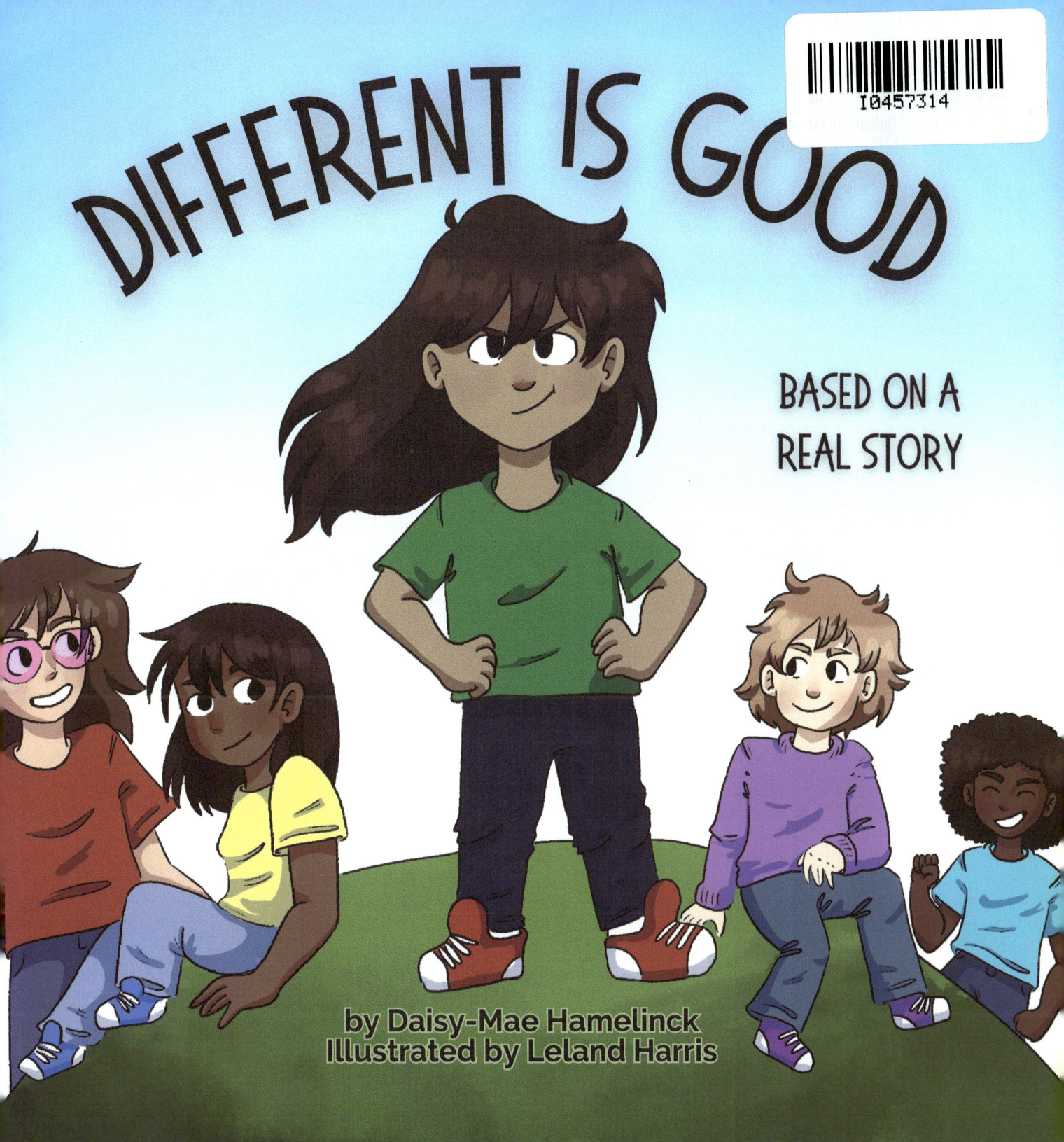

DIFFERENT IS GOOD

BASED ON A REAL STORY

by Daisy-Mae Hamelinck
Illustrated by Leland Harris

Twin Horseshoes Publishing
www.twinhorseshoes.ca
Ontario, Canada

Daisy-Mae Hamelinck and Leland Harris
Different is Good
Includes bibliographical references.

Paperback ISBN 978-1-990831-04-1
Hardcover ISBN 978-1-990831-05-8
eBook ISBN 978-1-990831-03-4

Juvenile Nonfiction | Social Topics | Prejudice & Racism
Juvenile Fiction | School & Education
Juvenile Nonfiction | Social Topics | Bullying

Themes: Gender, Class, Travel, Culture, Family, Diversity, Media

DEDICATION

This book is dedicated to YOU the reader—young or old.
May you embrace YOUR story and all that YOU are.

- Daisy

This book belongs to:

For my mom, who always pushed me to be the best I could be.

- Leland

Not too long ago, a baby girl was born.
Her name was Daisy-Mae.

Daisy-Mae had a mom and a dad who came to Canada from two
different countries, the Philippines and the Netherlands.

One day, Daisy-Mae
got a baby sister. They
all lived in a unique house,
but she didn't like it because
it was "different".

There were a lot of things Daisy-Mae didn't like.
Her mom told her to act like a lady, but she didn't want to
wear pink frilly dresses!

Instead, she wanted to get really dirty and play with big red trucks, so she did.

Then Daisy-Mae went to school.

In grade one, she found out she was "different".
A boy in her class told her she didn't look like everyone else.

In grade six, she was told she was "different"...again.

A girl in her class told her she didn't have the same things as everyone else...and that she didn't belong.

This made her sad.

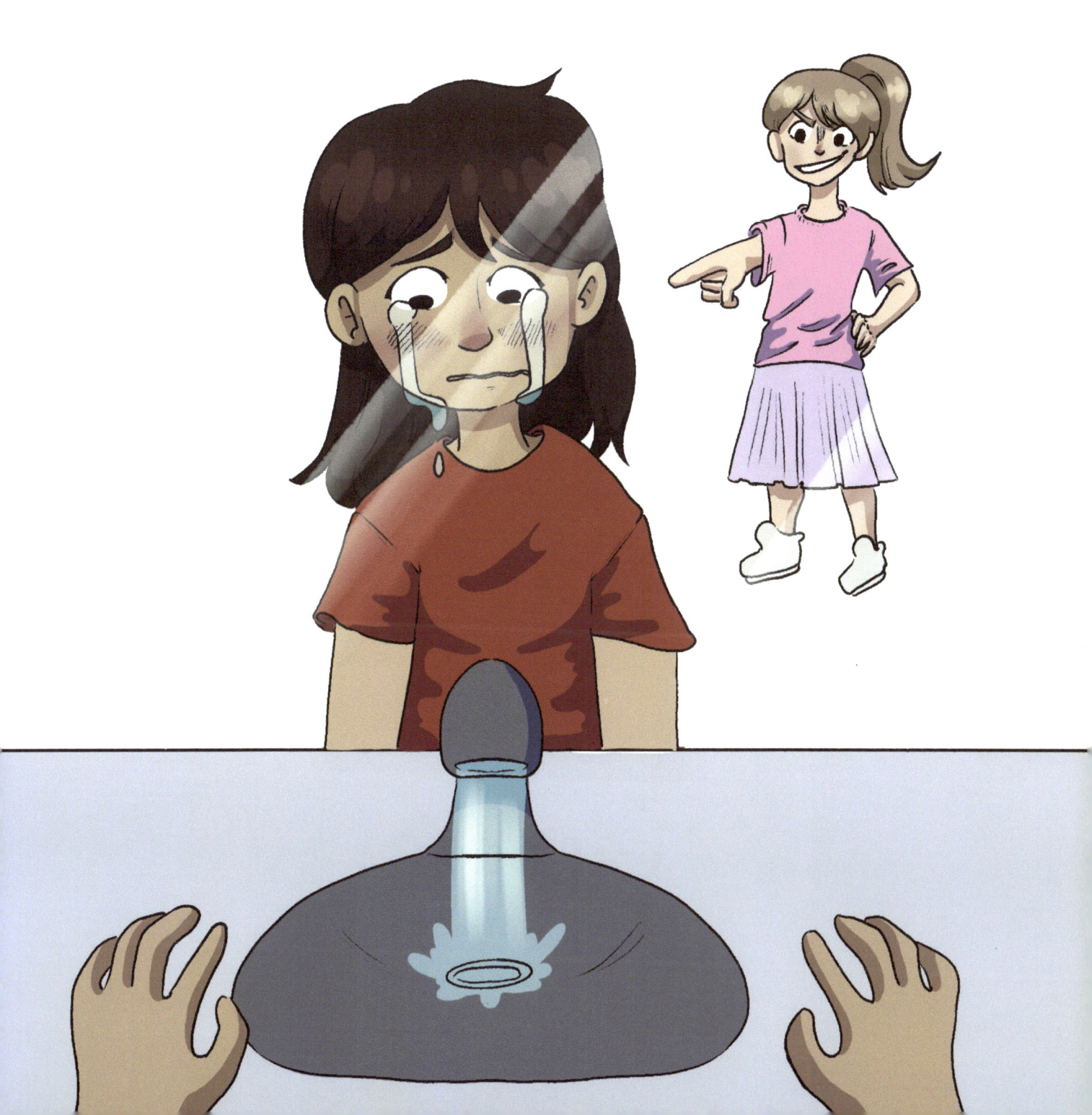

Daisy-Mae didn't like being different, so she tried to be like other people.

She didn't like her nose...or her eyes...she didn't even like her name. So, she tried to fix them.

Because she was being told she was "different", Daisy-Mae didn't know how to act.

Her mom and dad didn't like when she wanted to do things her own way.

Sometimes they would fight.
Her family didn't know how to show their feelings and be affectionate with each other.

This made it hard for them to get along.

Her mom told her to act a certain way...her dad told her to act a certain way...her friends told her to act a certain way. Even her TV told her to act a certain way.

She was so confused.

Her mom and dad didn't know what to do.
So, they sent her to a private school.
She did not like it very much.

Then she finally got to go to a school she did like.

One day, Daisy-Mae went on an airplane to visit another country called the Philippines. She had family there.

She learned lots of things on her trip...

She was the same person, but instead of being made fun of, everyone loved her.

Daisy-Mae didn't feel so bad about herself anymore.

When Daisy-Mae came home from her trip, she knew
she wanted to act in her own way.
So, she did.

When her friends were being mean to others, she wasn't.
When her friends didn't want to play with
the new girl at school, she did.

It made her happy.

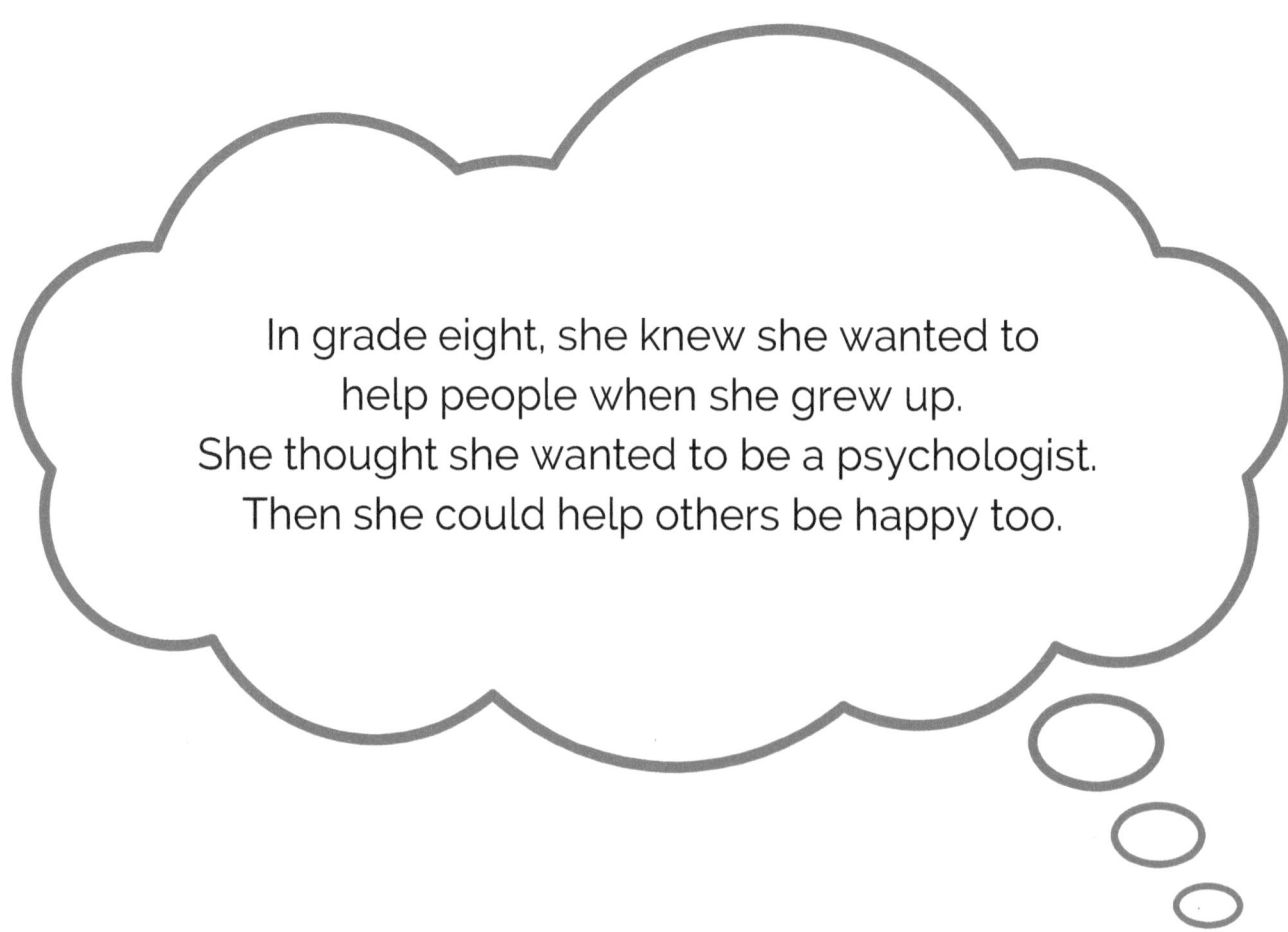

In grade eight, she knew she wanted to
help people when she grew up.
She thought she wanted to be a psychologist.
Then she could help others be happy too.

She began helping people who needed a little extra help.

Then she met a really good friend. He helped her
learn how to show her feelings.
She was ready to live in a new place. She stayed with her friend's
family and they were like a second family to her.

She moved to a new city and went to a big school where she
would learn to be a psychologist.
Then she decided she wanted to be a teacher.

While she was at school, some children showed her that maybe
she should be a social worker.
She moved again and went to another school.

She really liked going to school and learning.
It helped her to understand the world.

Sometimes she was too busy with school to visit her parents.
Maybe she also blamed them for trying to make her
into someone different.

But it wasn't their fault, just like it wasn't her fault that
she wanted to be herself.

She felt sad for fighting with her parents.
She wanted to tell them nice things, so she did.

Then she thought about things some more.

Her family helped make her who she was, and she was happy to be different.

She was unique!

There was absolutely no one like Daisy-Mae.
She liked her nose, her eyes, and even her name.
Being different was good.

"All these things are special because they belong to me!"

Daisy-Mae wants YOU to know that
YOU are different, unique, and special too!

WHAT DO YOU LIKE ABOUT YOURSELF?

List the unique and special qualities that
YOU like about yourself!

DRAW A PICTURE OF YOURSELF!

BASED ON A REAL STORY

"Different is Good" was written in 2003 as an assignment for a class in the Social Service Worker program at Fanshawe College. The first draft of this book sat in storage for 20 years.

The book tells some of the impactful experiences in the author's life up until 2003. These experiences still shape her daily interactions—whether it be in the classroom, get togethers with friends, or with strangers that pass in the moment.

"Different is Good" aims to remind the reader that we all have something that will make us "feel different," BUT it is how we embrace that difference that counts. The book presents themes of race, class, gender, ability, bullying, body acceptance, forgiveness, generosity, courage, and bravery.

ABOUT THE TEAM

We are all different too! This project was a true collaboration of individuals each bringing their own differences to the team. We represent neurodiverse, visible minority, transgendered, infertility, physical and mental health challenged, and cancer surviving populations. The best way to celebrate our differences is to talk about them with each other!

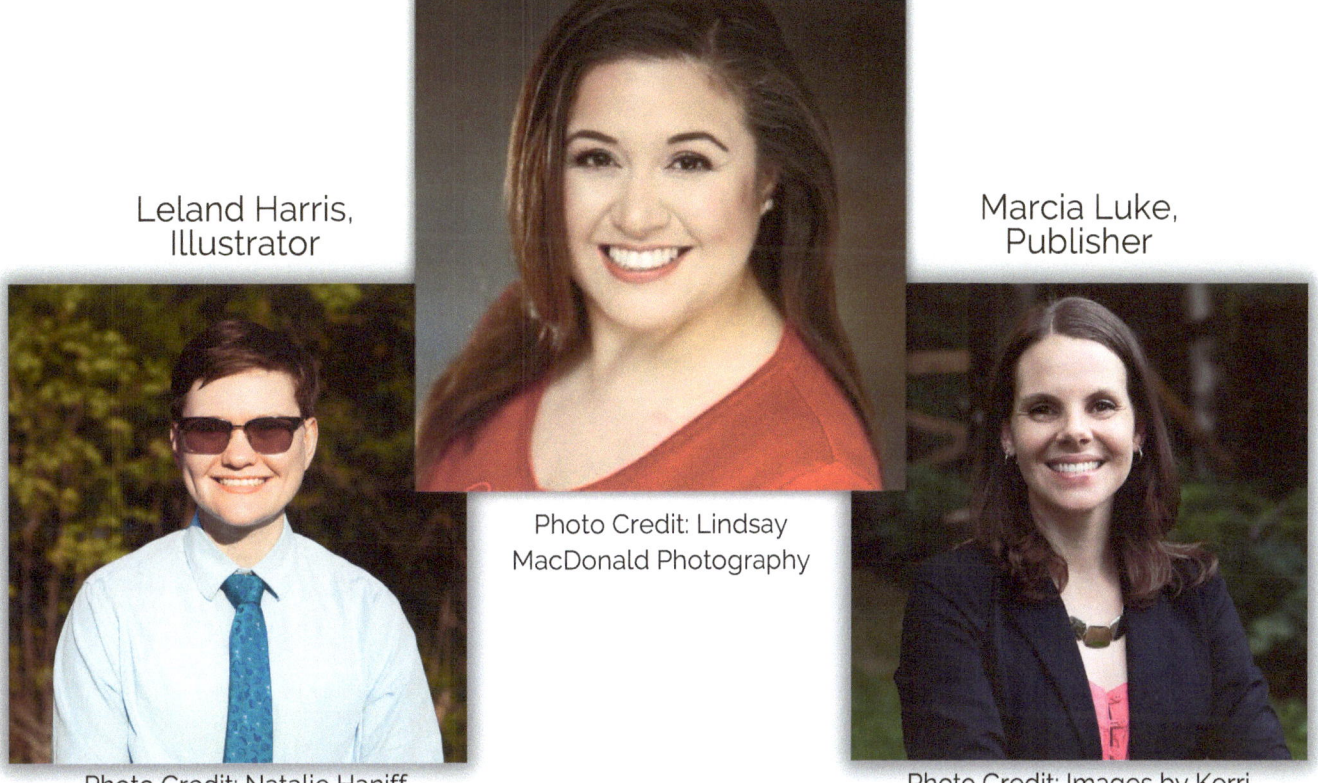

Daisy-Mae Hamelinck,
Author

Leland Harris,
Illustrator

Marcia Luke,
Publisher

Photo Credit: Lindsay
MacDonald Photography

Photo Credit: Natalie Haniff

Photo Credit: Images by Kerri

ABOUT THE AUTHOR

Daisy-Mae Hamelinck completed her Master of Arts in the Department of Sociology at McMaster University. She holds an Honours Bachelor of Arts (Wilfrid Laurier University), Bachelor of Education-Primary/Junior (University of Toronto), and a Social Service Worker Diploma (Fanshawe). Daisy's first co-authored book, "Interpersonal and Group Dynamics: A Practical Guide to Building an Effective Team" (3rd Edition) was published in 2018 and is currently used in colleges across Canada. Daisy has taught for 20+ years in post-secondary settings and is currently teaching at Fanshawe College and Western University.

As a two-time cancer survivor, Daisy has presented regularly with the Terry Fox Foundation and the Canadian Medical Hall of Fame. She has appeared on local TV stations to discuss her health journey. In 2020, she was diagnosed with Irlen Syndrome. It is through these experiences that she often raises awareness and speaks about the Accessibility for Ontarians with Disabilities Act (AODA). She is also a primary caregiver for two aging parents with various mental and physical health issues. Daisy keeps herself balanced by spending time with loved ones, practicing yoga and meditation, attending church regularly, and travelling nationally/internationally.

Daisy strives to live her best life and enables others to do the same through workshops and one-on-one sessions at her success coaching business, Your New Leaf. She helps participants develop life skills, set and achieve goals, and engage in creative problem solving using the 8 dimensions of wellness.

ACKNOWLEDGEMENTS

To Marcia: For always making all my ideas come to life, literally in a matter of minutes. I am in awe of you. Cheers to the alpaca magic. Let's keep being the horse chasing that cart.

To Leland: For the amazing illustrations in this book and the ability to take my amateur drawings and put to paper what was actually in my head all along.

To my friends and loved ones (aka cheerleaders): I am so fortunate to have you all in my life along my journey. I am a friend and chosen-family collector, and I am happy to say that I have "cream of the crop" people in my circle. Thank you for always rooting for me and all that I do.

To the people and places mentioned in this book AND the ups and downs along the way: You have shaped my life story that I tell to this day. These experiences have influenced my interactions on a daily basis, personally, and professionally., The impact goes far and wide.

To my higher power: Thank you for helping me live my passion and purpose.

ABOUT THE ILLUSTRATOR

Leland Harris has been drawing for as long as he can remember. As a kid, he would go to the library and check out as many "how to draw" books as he could carry. Nowadays, he's busy completing his Bachelor's of Music and starting his Bachelor's of Education, with the dream of teaching music or art. In his spare time, he likes to write music, crochet, and of course, draw.

As a transgender person, he is very excited to share the message that "Different is Good", especially to every kid who feels different from everyone else. He has found joy in his different-ness, and hopes that everyone reading will as well.

ACKNOWLEDGEMENTS

This book wouldn't have been possible without my parents who always supported my art and my passions. They have set me up to succeed through everything they have done for me.

ABOUT THE PUBLISHER

Marcia Allyn Luke has a Master of Professional Education, Curriculum & Pedagogy from Western University, an Honours Bachelor in English from the University of Guelph, and a postgraduate Publishing Certificate from Ryerson University.

Marcia has 17 years' experience in post-secondary education and publishing in a variety of teaching, editorial, sales, marketing, project management, acquisitions, and new program development positions, providing a unique, holistic perspective. She has been a writer at heart from the very beginning, writing children's books for younger grades in elementary school. Marcia has authored and published a memoir, "Letters to My Hypothetical Children", contributed to a #1 internationally bestselling book, "Silent Grief, Healing, & Hope", and written numerous articles for TWINS Magazine, New Dreamhomes Magazine, and Life in Multiples. Marcia is currently the Vice President, National Executive Council for Editors Canada.

In addition to teaching, Marcia has her own publishing business, Twin Horseshoes, helping people fulfill their dream of being a published author. The Twin Horseshoes philosophy is that by publishing authentic, diverse stories we can make the world a kinder place to live. Outside of work, Marcia is a mom to twin girls. She likes reading, spending time with family and friends, rock climbing, and participating in any activity outside.

FIND THE LEAVES

Throughout the book, there are **ten** pages with hidden leaves to prompt conversation about the below topics and indicate additional resources available for children, teachers, and parents. Find the leaves and go to yournewleaf.ca/find-the-leaves to access resources on the following topics:

- diversity/race/ethnicity
- socioeconomic status
- gender
- education
- ability
- family dynamics
- health
- body image
- media
- bullying
- travel
- career/profession
- friendship

www.ingramcontent.com/pod-product-compliance
Lightning Source LLC
Chambersburg PA
CBHW041618120626
46551CB00003B/495